Jo Draper has been researching on Dorset for thirty years. She was Editor of the *Proceedings of the Dorset Natural History & Archaeological Society* for fifteen years, and has written several books on the county including *Dorset: the Complete Guide, Dorset Food* and three books on Dorchester. With John Fowles she wrote *Thomas Hardy's England.* She lives in Dorchester with her husband, with whom she wrote *Walking Dorset History.* She is also the author of *The Georgians* in the 'Discover Dorset' series.

*Following page*
Robert Gooden's memorial figure at Over Compton was put up by the man himself three years before his death, aged 77, in 1828. It is a wonderful example of the realism of many Regency memorials. Gooden was a bachelor and landowner, and he really looks the part. Hutchins says the figure shows him 'attired in his accustomed homely dress'.

ROBERT GOODDEN
BORN IN THIS PARISH
THE FOURTEENTH OF AUGUST
1751.
BEAUTIFIED THIS CHURCH
1822.
THIS STATUE EXECUTED
1823.
DIED THE THIRD OF OCTOBER
1828.

DISCOVER DORSET

# REGENCY,
# RIOT AND REFORM

JO DRAPER

THE DOVECOTE PRESS

An ordinary Dorset village through Romantic
early nineteenth century eyes. Lulworth engraved in 1828.

First published in 2000 by The Dovecote Press Ltd
Stanbridge, Wimborne, Dorset BH21 4JD

ISBN 1 874336 70 9

Series designed by Humphrey Stone

Typeset in Sabon by The Typesetting Bureau
Wimborne, Dorset
Printed and bound by Baskerville Press, Salisbury, Wiltshire

A CIP catalogue record for this book is available
from the British Library

1 3 5 7 9 8 6 4 2

# CONTENTS

INTRODUCTION 7

THE COUNTY 10

CHANGES IN FARMING 30

THE LABOURERS 41

CHURCH AND CHAPEL 55

THE POORLAW AND THE WORKHOUSE 68

THE TOLPUDDLE MARTYRS 72

THE REGENCY LEGACY 77

FURTHER READING 78

ACKNOWLEDGEMENTS 79

DEVO
of Dorset
HIRE
Stockland
Axminster
Lyme Regis
Chard
Lambert's Castle
Pen Inn
Three Ashes
Charmouth
Rising Sun
Crewkherne
Broad
Chidiock
Winsor
Bridport
E.Dibberford
Perrot
Morterton
Netherbury
Beaminster
Chedington
Yeovil
Bradpole
Hoole
Melbury Sampford
Evershot
Abbotsbury
Chilfrome
Sherborne
to Marston Magna & Castle Cary
Maiden Newton
Frampton
to Wincaunton
Long Burton
Oborn
Winterborn Abbas
Winterborn Steplton
Cerne Abbas
Milborne Port
Winterborn St Martins
Charminster
Stalbridge Park
Portland Bill or Point
Weymouth
Winterborn Monkton
Dorchester
Henstridge
to Wincaunton & Castle Cary
Broad Maine
Warmwell
Tincleton
Stalbridge
Kimeridge Bay
Osmington
Galton
Piddle
Milton Abby
Sturminster
Stower Provost
Gillingham
Worth Barrow B.
Winfrith Newburgh
Milborn St Andrew
Stower Eastover
Encombe Bay
Bere Regis
Winterborn Whitchurch
Shaftsbury
St Aldan's H.
Stowborough
Watchim
Blandford St Mary
Brownstone Place
to Salisbury the London Rd
Corfe Castle
Lytchet Minster
Charlton Marshall
Spettisbury
Blandford Forum
Langton Matravers
Corfe Mullen
Pimpern
Eastbury House
Chettle
Swanage
Sturminster Marshall
Gussage
More Critchill
Cashmoor Inn
Morley
Poole
Wimborn Minster
Horton
Cranbourn
Kingston
Langham
Bournes
Iwberne
to Salisbury the London Rd

CHANNEL
ENGLISH
SOMERSET
WILTS
HAMPSHIRE

London to Cranbourn 92 Wimborn Minster 101 Poole 106 Corfe Castle 120 Wareham 115 Blandford 103
Shaftsbury 101 Bere Regis 113 Milton Abby 111 Sturminster 111 Stalbridge 113 Weymouth 128 Melcombe Regis 127
Dorchester 120 Frampton 126 Cerne Abbas 120 Sherborne 117 Evershot 135 Bridport 134 Lyme Regis 143
Abbotsbury 130 Beaminster 137.

London Published July 1 1806 by J. Cary Engraver N.º 181 Strand.

# INTRODUCTION

'It was judged necessary to block up all the lower windows of Moreton House, as well as all the doors, with the exception of that to the offices. The Mayor of Dorchester ordered the staff of Dorset Militia to go to Moreton to defend the house, nightly patrols were established, and Mr Frampton or his son sat up alternately for many nights. My sister-in-law also took her turn in sitting up with another woman, Lady Harriot saying that they were more watchful than men.'

Mary Frampton is writing about Dorset in November 1830. The enemy the big house was being defended against was not the French or the Germans, but the working class farm-labourers of the district, who were setting fire to hay and corn ricks and destroying the new threshing machines which were taking away their usual winter work. Troops were employed against them in Dorset (and other counties) and many of the upper and middle classes thought that England was about to have a revolution like the one France had suffered less than forty years earlier. A poem distributed in Blandford in about 1831 summarises the problem:

*And if we do not have Reform*
*We'll soon have Revolution*

Moreton House, and its owner James Frampton, were targets

Dorset in 1810, turned unfamiliarly with north to the right. The major coaching routes dominate. The map-maker has mostly shown the turnpike roads, which were much better than the others. The stars giving the number of MPs from each place shows pre-Reform Corfe still with two. Cranborne was left off the main coaching routes, and was starting to decline. Dorchester's nodal position on important roads shows clearly.

because Frampton was a prominent opponent of the labourers. He was going to be important in the climax of Dorset's troubles – the trial of the Tolpuddle Martyrs – four years later.

The history of Regency Dorset shows the forces and changes which led up to these confrontations of 1830, and how the county (and country) recovered from it.

The legal Regency, when the Prince of Wales (later George IV) acted as regent for George III, lasted only nine years from 1811, but the term is often used in a wider sense, to cover the period from around 1800 to the end of George IV's reign in 1830, or even up to Victoria's accession in 1837. This was a period of enormous change in the whole country, and Dorset played a prominent role because of the Tolpuddle Martyrs. The whole period 1800-1837 will be considered

George IV parodied 'Mr George King - the Parish Overseer' in 1829. As Prince of Wales, George had rented Crichel in north Dorset for hunting, but he preferred Brighton to Weymouth for seaside residence.

Looking down High West Street, Dorchester in the 1830s. The artist has shown a mixture of men to symbolise the town: a corpulent tradesman; a richly dressed soldier on his horse and two young men with another soldier. The barracks were close by, and the soldiers add an exotic touch.

here because it makes much more sense to see the full background to the problems of the agricultural labourers, and its outcome.

The background to the struggles of the Dorsetshire labourers is complex. Their concerns are thrown into sharper relief because simultaneously Dorset's upper and middle classes were becoming richer – most of them (the farmers and landowners) at the expense of those same agricultural labourers.

Even Dorset's physical appearance was changing. Many fashionable new buildings were erected, and there were significant alterations to the landscape itself through enclosure and other farming improvements. Ironically, alongside these changes, appreciation of the landscape (particularly wild landscapes) was growing with the Romantic movement. Earlier, only useful and profitable land had been admired: now wild areas were the fashion. The Dorset coast was just the sort of picturesque (literally suitable for painting) and dramatic scenery that was then desired.

# THE COUNTY

In 1800 Dorset was a rural county, with about 260 villages, each of which had 5-10 farms. The eleven inland towns were agricultural centres. Two of the four coastal towns (Poole and Swanage) were ports but the other two (Weymouth and Lyme Regis) were the most fashionable and stylish settlements because they were watering places.

In 1801 the first census was taken, so the number of inhabitants in the county is known accurately for the first time. Dorset had 114,452 people, only twice as many as live in Weymouth and Portland today. In 1801 there was less than one person per 5 acres. By 1841 there were 175,274 people, half as many again. Impressive though the increase is, the population of the whole of England and Wales had nearly doubled over the same priod to reach 16 million in 1841.

Blandford Races in August 1818. Horse racing was then very popular, and Dorset had several annual races like this one which disappeared later in the century. The Dorsetshire Gold Cup of 100 guineas was the main prize at Blandford. A ball followed the first days racing, 'attended by upwards of 140 of the youth, beauty and fashion of the county' (*Sherborne Mercury*).

An early nineteenth century villa on the outskirts of Bridport. Many villas were built on the edges of towns at this time, some quite small and in the new semi-detached style. The decorative cast-iron gate and piers are original.

In 1801 two-thirds of the inhabitants of Dorset lived in villages and hamlets, and this proportion changed only slightly over the next forty years. The eleven inland towns grew by about the average proportion over the period, as did Swanage and Dorset's largest town – Poole. The two other seaside towns – Weymouth and Lyme Regis – had become resorts, and both more than doubled their population, Weymouth having more people than Poole in 1841 for the first time.

The greatest growth took place in suburbs: Fordington, the village adjacent to Dorchester grew from 888 people in 1801 to 2,937 in 1841, and at Bridport Allington increased from 716 to 1,746 and Bradpole from 575 to 1,357. At Weymouth, the adjoining rural parish of Wyke Regis showed the largest increase in the county, from 451 to 1,911. Fordington grew because so many displaced farm labourers moved there. Taxes were solely on property, so no landowner or farmer wanted to maintain more cottages than were required to house their labourers. In order to rent a home the displaced labourers had to move to the towns. Enclosure and other problems reduced the numbers of labourers needed, and increased the numbers of poor in the towns and suburbs. Bradpole and Allington also grew because the net and rope industry thrived during the Napoleonic wars.

Virtually everyone outside the towns was employed in agriculture, and even the inland towns were there to supply the farmers and market their produce. The Industrial Revolution, with the transfer of manufacture from single craftsmen to the large factory, had already started in the north and midlands. Regency Dorset, lacking natural resources such as coal and iron-ore, was left behind by industrialisation, and remained a rural backwater, but at the time many of the inhabitants assumed that Dorset would develop industries.

The wars against France were only part of the turmoil. Religious and political divisions were becoming more extreme, and generally society was more violent. Gangs of smugglers and poachers were not

An engraving by William Barnes of Mr Thomas' bookshop at Weymouth. It was built in about 1800 as Harvey's Library and Card Assembly. The Library (which also sold books) was on the ground floor, the assembly room on the first. The Ionic capitals to the pillars and the decorative glazing bars on the windows above the doors are typical of many buildings of around 1800.

Some industrialisation took place in Dorset. The Merchant's Railway, Portland, was the second railway built in Dorset – the first was at Norden in 1806, built to transport clay from the quarries to Poole Harbour. Like the Norden one, the Portland railway of 1826 was powered by horses: steam locomotives had not yet been invented. The drawing shows the most spectacular part of the railway – the incline which brought the stone down the steep slope and to the harbour. The railway was so successful that in a single day in June 1828, 300 tons of stone were carried from the quarries to the ships (*The Dorset County Chronicle*).

uncommon, and justice was still savage, with the death penalty for small offences. Until 1808 picking pockets, stealing goods worth 5s (25p) from a shop, horse-stealing and burglary were hanging offences. After 1838 only murder carried the death penalty. The lives of the farm labourers and their families were getting harder, and a new middle class of tradesmen and farmers was emerging. During the 1831 county election at Dorchester (fought largely on the issue of reform in Parliament) a local landowner remarked that 'since 1780 there has been a middle class produced, and brought into existence, between the higher and lower orders, who are entitled to rights'. This new middle class, along with the new non-conformists, was behind much of the drive for reform which characterises the period.

Regency Weymouth. Devonshire Buildings, right on the sea front. Until the later eighteenth century seaside towns turned their backs to the sea, but when some of them (like Weymouth) developed as resorts, houses were built facing the shore. The rounded end to the terrace is typical of Regency, as are the shallow bay windows.

More rounded corners at Weymouth, this time making a fine entrance to St Mary Street. The houses were built around 1810, and the huge statue of George III was placed here in 1809, five years after his last visit. The whole ensemble shows the Regency happily using one material to imitate another – the houses are not stone, but rendered in stucco to look like stone, and the statue is of artificial Coade stone.

A satirical print of bathing at Lyme Regis in 1818; the original caption is 'Hydromania! or a Touch of the Sub Lyme and Beautiful'. Women did not bathe naked in Regency Dorset, but the bathing machines are realistic.

## THE COAST AND RESORTS

Dorset had two elegant watering places – Weymouth and Lyme Regis. Both grew because the wars with France made travel abroad difficult, and more people took holidays in England. Britain was at war virtually without respite from 1793-1815.

George III continued to visit Weymouth until 1805, having made it one of England's most fashionable resorts by coming regularly from 1789. The town grew enormously over the period of the King's visits, and continued to grow even after he was unable to come because of his madness. Princess Charlotte, George IV's daughter and heir, visited Weymouth in 1814 and 1815. The mayor expressed the joy of the inhabitants at her arrival 'not only as a happy omen for the future prosperity of the town, but as a revival of the joyful sensations we formerly experienced on the visits of your august grandfather'.

Alas, Charlotte died in childbirth in 1817, and Weymouth's Royal days were over. After George III's death in 1820 the contents of Royal Lodge were sold by auction, followed by the house itself. In 1826 *The Dorset County Chronicle* lamented the 'melancholy charm' of the Theatre Royal, Weymouth, which was enhanced by the 'once

Bridport Harbour (now West Bay) engraved for William Daniell's *A Voyage Round Great Britain* (1825). The smaller ports thrived in the early nineteenth century: West Bay's entrance and harbour was deepened in 1823-5, and the piers extended.

regal box' where 'that revered and almost idolised father of his people, the late King [George III] has sat to witness the rational and innocent amusements of the theatre'.

Even in these elegant resorts there was law-breaking. Smuggling was common, and many inland Dorset labourers helped to carry the smuggled goods on to their final destinations. During the wars smuggling was at its greatest extent, but new laws and better policing started in 1816, when the Royal Navy took over the ships which monitored the coasts.

In December 1819 the Revenue cutter at Weymouth caught three smuggling ships in one day, loaded with 298 casks of spirits and 3 casks of tea. The next day the small Revenue boat went out in a strong gale and was overturned. The Revenue cutter and other boats, 'some manned by smugglers', immediately set off to the rescue, and saved four out of the five men. Smugglers were almost always superb sailors, and were often involved in rescues.

The war between the smugglers and the Preventative Service was

On Poole Quay the Harbour Office (left) was built in 1822, with typical plain classical detailing and an open colonnade. The Custom House (centre) was rebuilt after a fire in 1813, and retained some of its Georgian style, although the curving stairs and central doorway are very Regency.

waged most fiercely in the 1820s. In September 1827 smugglers were seen actually on the Esplanade at Weymouth, 'landing a quantity of Foreign Spirits from a boat'. When one of the Preventative men fired his pistol as a signal to his fellow officers the smugglers 'committed a violent assault' on him, 'knocking him down and beating him with Bludgeons'.

Spirits – brandy, gin and rum – were commonly smuggled. Tea was another staple, and wine, silks, snuff, lace, coffee, cocoa and even playing cards were regularly smuggled through Dorset. Thomas Hardy recorded that his grandfather was involved in smuggling at Bockhampton early in the nineteenth century, storing tubs of brandy in an out-house at his lonely cottage, and even in the 1830s the family was still supplied with smuggled spirits. By the end of that decade, with the reduction of duties on many items and stiffer laws against smugglers, the trade was virtually wiped out.

All the current Dorset towns existed in the Regency period, except Bournemouth, which was in its infancy as a tiny watering-place. Cooke's *Description of Dorset* (1836) noted a steam-driven soda water manufactory in Dorchester where the machinery 'and the new and extensive building are amongst the most complete works of the kind in the Kingdom', but in his general survey he had to admit that Dorset towns had 'manufacturing establishments on a small scale, yet, taken altogether this county does not rate high as a manufacturing station'.

Villas were built on the outskirts of all the Dorset towns in the Regency, but Bridport has more than most places. They housed the middle classes, and the very name villa suggests their style – middle sized, classically styled houses in their own grounds (which were sometimes, as here, very small). This one, in Charmouth Road, is characteristically plain in construction and stuccoed, but had elaborate ironwork on the verandah.

Buildings constructed as offices for the newly-expanding banks were a feature of many towns. They tend to be classical in style, solid and respectable looking. The pedimented building, which survives in High West Street, Dorchester, was built for the Dorsetshire Old Bank about 1834.

The Theatre Royal, North Square, Dorchester, was built in 1813. It was a small and simple building, one of two small theatres in the town used by travelling theatrical companies. This drawing, from the later nineteenth century, shows the building after it had become a Salvation Army Barracks.

Shaftesbury Town Hall (1826) is in the solid late medieval style sometimes used for Regency public buildings.

The towns remained the rural centres they had always been, although the shops were becoming more sophisticated and organisations like banks more common.

Apart from affrays with smugglers or poachers, it was in the towns that most of the rioting happened. There were simply more people, and seasonal celebrations like Christmas, Guy Fawkes Day and fairs often ended in drunken riots. Elections were perhaps the worst, helped along by some of the bribery being in drink, and the obvious sides to be taken. In 1829 *The Dorset County Chronicle* reported 'A Christmas Frolic' when a 'party of soldiers were drinking in the Three Mariners public house' Dorchester, with several townsmen and others from Fordington. 'A dispute having arisen on some trivial topic, words soon gave way to blows, and the soldiers, drawing their swords, attacked the townsmen without distinction, and wounded several very seriously. The others procured spits, pokers, pitchforks, or any other weapon they could lay their hands on, and a general melée ensured'. The soldiers retreated up the High Street towards the barracks 'cutting at everyone in their progress, and pelted by the populace with stones etc.'. The paper was surprised that no-one was killed.

The 1826 Weymouth election was worse than most: a drunken (and hired) mob invaded the Town Hall 'hustled the freeholders from the place of polling, got on the table of the court, endeavored to pull the Mayor from his chair, and committed the most daring outrages' to prevent the voting from continuing. The Mayor escaped through a back door as the building was damaged, 'the Riot Act was read, and an express was despatched to Dorchester for the military'. This was the usual ending to most riots; there was no police force so the army was the only enforcer. Sadly, the candidate who employed the mob won the election.

THE TOWNS AND REFORM. John Penny, editor of *The Sherborne Journal*, published a pamphlet in 1833 on the need to reduce taxation, and the start is typical of the period, 'since our age is in the humour to reform abuses, and the country has set about examining the defects and repairing the damage which our constitution has received from the accidents of time, or the encroachments of power,'

---

TO THE

# BOROUGHMONGERS

# OF DORSET

## And Elsewhere.

Your reign is past, the glorious fight is won,
In vain you strive---REFORM'S full tide rolls on,
As o'er the land like some vast flood it flows,
Strong from a thousand generous springs it grows,
Retire in time!!! before its awful force,
Nor trust to feeble BANKS to stop its course.

---

Poster of 1831, printed in Lyme Regis. Banks was Henry Bankes, one of the Tory (and anti-Reform) candidates in the May county election, 1831. He was defeated, and two pro-Reform candidates were sent to Parliament from Dorset. This poster must have been part of the victory celebrations.

# Electors

OF

# *ENGLAND,*

*You are to decide by YOUR VOTES between*

| OLD England. | NEW England. |
|---|---|
| The Institutions of your fore-fathers. | The Institutions which a French-hearted MINISTRY would cram down your throats |
| A system under which, by God's blessing, you have been the happiest, richest, and freest nation under Heaven. | A system which wherever it has been tried, has brought confusion and desolation. |
| Your English Constitution which has stood the test of Ages | A new Foreign Constitution, of which the little that is known is evil. |
| A system which secures to every individual in the Kingdom, every right he ever possessed. | A system which begins by depriving 150,000 Voters of their undoubted right. |
| *English Ascendancy.* *Church of England.* *Peace,* *A Monarchy.* *Security.* *Prosperity.* *Freedom.* | *Irish Ascendancy.* *No Church.* *Civil War.* *A Republic.* *Spoliation.* *Ruin.* *Military Despotism.* |
| Those who are on this side will Vote AGAINST THE REFORM BILL. | Those who are on this side will Vote FOR THE REFORM BILL. |

Anti-Reform poster from the second county election in 1831.
Reform is French, and will lead to a revolution like the French one;
the Irish will rule and all will be ruined.

An unusual memorial – Reform Place, Allington, a terrace of small houses named to commemorate the 1835 Municipal Reform Act which changed the old corrupt town councils into elected bodies.

now is the time to remove or reform the cause of all distress – namely taxation.

Penny was writing after Parliament itself had been changed by the Reform Act of 1832. The Act removed the right from tiny places like Corfe Castle to elect MPs, and extended the number from the growing northern manufacturing towns. To the disappointment of many reformers, the qualification for voting was still based on property, so although the number of voters nearly doubled, it remained a small minority. Universal Suffrage – one man, one vote – was still nearly a century away. The towns were themselves reformed in 1835 by yet another Reform Act. In place of the old system whereby the Corporations who ran the Boroughs chose new members themselves, Borough Councils were to be elected by all the Poor Rate payers of the town.

Dorset was split on the need for parliamentary reform – George Bankes of Kingston Lacy, as candidate for the county seat in 1826 repeated the Conservative view, 'I am firmly attached to our excellent Constitution in Church and State as it present stands and as it was settled at the Revolution [the Conservatives made much of the 'revolution' of 1688 – if England had already had a revolution, reform wasn't needed]. Let those who would wish to make innovations amuse themselves with the experiment: I am perfectly content with what our ancestors have left in our hands'. Innovation, experiment and reform can be left to foreigners, like the French. Church and State are one indivisible entity.

TOWN SOCIETIES. Many new societies were established to improve or change social or religious problems, and all towns developed a huge range. In Dorchester in 1827 there were eight, which had all been established since 1811. Half were branches of national societies: the Ladies' Association for Promoting Christianity among the Jews, the Ladies' Bible Association, the Society for Promoting Christian Knowledge and the Church Missionary Society, but the others were local. A Society for the Suppression of Mendicity was established to remove beggars from the town: in 1826 it had helped 517 people, refused help to 33 more as not deserving it, and punished 4 people as 'imposters'. The Charitable Institution helped 'poor married women during their confinement' and supplied 'old and infirm persons with necessary clothing'. The Savings Bank was to give 'the industrious classes' a safe place to save money. The Shipwreck Society covered the whole county, and raised funds for lifeboats.

The emphasis in all eight societies was a single word: 'deserving'. Even the aged were only to be given 'necessary' clothing, and unmarried mothers were not even mentioned. Self-help was the aim of the Savings Bank, and generally the tone of the societies was that of the new industrious, Anglican middle class.

Public coaches reached their peak in the Regency, before competition from the railways started. In 1832 coaches called at Dorchester 96 times a week – sixteen a day, as none ran on Sundays. Three ran daily to and from London, one from Southampton, one from Bristol or Bath and one linking Portsmouth to Exeter. At least four of these services continued to Weymouth, and there was also a daily coach running between Dorchester and Weymouth.

Robert Southey, the poet, published a book of *Letters from England* (1808) which purported to be by a Spaniard. In it he described seeing a coach in Dorset:

> One passed us this morning, shaped like a trunk with a rounded lid placed topsy-turvy. The passengers sit sideways; it

A bill dated 1835, from William Meaden, Coach Builder and Harness Maker. The three vehicles which decorate his bill-head are a phaeton (left) carrying four people; a chariot (top) a cut-down coach with only one seat inside and a separate seat for the driver; and a gig (right) which seated two. The chariot had a coachman, but the other two were driven by the owner.
The three vehicles represent the range used by the wealthy, omitting the larger coaches used for public transport.

carries sixteen persons withinside, and as many on the roof as can find room; yet this unmerciful weight with the proportionate luggage of each person is dragged by four horses, at the rate of a league and a half within the hour [about 4½ miles an hour]. The skill with which the driver guides them with long reins, and directs these huge machines round the corners of the streets where they always go with increased velocity, and through the sharp turns of the inn gateways, is truly surprising. Accidents nevertheless frequently happen; and considering how

The Antelope, South Street, Dorchester, a coaching inn refronted in the early nineteenth century. The big shallow bays with three windows in each are unusually large. The windows on the first floor run right to the ground to allow access to the pretty iron balcony. Many coaching inns were rebuilt in the early nineteenth century because that was the peak of coach transport.

The New Inn, Sherborne, is a huge contrast to the Antelope. The engraving was made in 1815, and is one of many produced in the early nineteenth century showing old buildings. Interest in earlier architecture was developing and becoming more informed. The New Inn dated from the late fifteenth century, and was demolished in the 1840s. Its stone mullioned windows and general 'ancient' air made it picturesque to Regency eyes.

little time this rapidity allows for observing the country, and how cruelly it is purchased, I prefer the slow and safe movements of the calessa [a one horse trap...]

The coaching inns provided both accommodation and stabling. In 1833 the Antelope, one of the two main coaching inns at Dorchester, was advertising itself as a 'Commercial Inn and Posting House' with very superior accommodation, and 'spacious, airy, quiet and commodious' bedrooms. Equally important was 'the Stabling' which was 'of a first rate description; experienced Ostlers are in attendance; the best Hay and Corn kept; and lock-up Coach Houses are attached'. 'Active and steady waiters' were ready to serve the humans meals 'with every production of the respective seasons'.

The fastest way to travel was by mail coach – the coaches which carried the mail. They were established in 1784, and two routes passed through Dorset: London to Devonport through Shaftesbury and London to Exeter through Dorchester. The mail coaches kept up a steady seven miles an hour, which was then regarded as miraculous.

Thomas Hardy remembered Kenfield, a neighbour at Bockhampton, who had been a guard of the mail coach from London to

The Horn Tunnel, Beaminster, about 1900. This road tunnel opened in 1832, and is a precursor of the railways which soon followed. Cooke's *Dorset* (1836) describes it as having 'a very commodious passage through the bowels of a high hill, and the Taunton and Bridport mail [coach] passes through it twice every day'. The tunnel is 115 yards long, and saves the road having to climb a further 100 feet. The tollhouse (since demolished) was an odd but impressive classical-like building.

Dorchester in the 1830s – 'He carried 2 pistols, a cutlass, a blunderbuss in a long tin box' and wore a uniform of 'a red frock-coat, with blue flaps to the pockets and a blue collar'. He was guard all the way from Dorchester to London, but there were two or three coachmen over the distance, and another guard took over for Dorchester-Exeter. The horses were changed more frequently, firstly at Blandford. The guard blew his horn at every place where the mail was taken up, and on his arrival at Dorchester he immediately took out the letter-bags and delivered them to the Post Office. Hardy was fascinated by a fiddle run by Kenfield: butter, eggs and game were packed into a hamper, and someone would be waiting near Bockhampton to give it to the coach, 'which pulled up for a moment to receive the hamper, and rolled on again'. Kenfield sold the goods in London, having illegally transported them.

The slowest long-distance transport were the wagons which carried

Telegraph Cottage at Chalbury was built in 1806, with weather-boarded walls, as a station on the London-Plymouth line for semaphore telegraph. Admiralty messages could be passed from London to Plymouth and back again in three minutes in ideal weather conditions. The shutters which passed the messages were held on a large wooden frame over the cottage. The line closed in 1816, after the war with France was won.

goods and passengers who could only afford the cheapest fares. They moved only a couple of miles an hour, less than walking pace. In 1827 five different firms were running wagons through Dorchester, with at least two a day leaving for London, Exeter, Bath (or Bristol) and more to Weymouth.

Travelling by coach, or even wagon, was much too expensive for the labourers: they walked. When the Tolpuddle Martyrs were arrested in February 1834 they 'walked in the company with the constable to Dorchester, about seven miles distant'. George Loveless mentions this in his account, not because of the walking (which was usual) but because of the constable.

Even pedestrians were vulnerable to robbers: in 1837 a labourer walked into Dorchester from a village ten miles out to visit his daughter who was in service at the George Inn and his son at the Barracks. On his return, they walked a mile up the road with him, but after they left he was attacked by two men who appeared from behind the hedge, robbed him of his silver watch and 4s 6d in money, and left him dying in the road from a tremendous blow with a bludgeon (*Dorset County Chronicle*).

# CHANGES IN FARMING

The Napoleonic Wars, which lasted from 1794 to 1815, had a huge effect on farming. Imports were completely stopped, and prices soared. A quarter of wheat (8 bushels or 480 lbs) averaged 50s (£2.50) before the wars; in February 1801 panic prices drove it to 200s (£10) at Dorchester, although by October it was down to 70s (£3.50). 100s or double the pre-war price, was usual during the period. Other crops also became more expensive. Hemp for ropes and flax for sail-cloth was grown in west Dorset in the late eighteenth century, but production increased enormously because the traditional suppliers in north Europe were cut off, and demand for the products soared because of the great expansion of the Navy.

High prices meant agriculture expanded and improved in a drive to produce more. Farmers made huge profits, and could afford to introduce new methods and machinery. Sir J. W. Smith, addressing a meeting in support of the Corn Laws at Blandford in 1826 lauded the farmer's work during the war:

> Most of us, now present, have lived in the period when the great Tyrant of France succeeded in shutting out our commerce from all the ports of the Continent; when, in consequence, wheat rose to the enormous price of £50 per load, and other grain in proportion; and when, but for the united exertions of the skill and capital of the agricultural body, in forcing into cultivation every acre of land capable of producing a blade of corn, this empire must have been subjected to all the horrors of famine.

Prices collapsed when the war ended. In 1813 wheat was averaging 100s (£5) a quarter, but in 1815 it fell to 65s (£3.25). The Corn Laws were formulated in 1815 to prevent the import of wheat unless the price here was at least 80s (£4) a quarter. The law was designed

A farm in Dorset, engraved in 1818. The artist has chosen it because of its picturesque qualities but it gives a realistic idea of a small farm, with the house on the right and farm buildings.

to protect farmers, and cut clean across ideas of free trade. With modifications, the laws remained in place until 1845. Even with this protection, farming was much less profitable.

Evidence given before the Select Committee on petitions complaining of the Depressed State of Agriculture (1831), included one from Mr William Ilott, a tenant farmer in Milton Abbas, showing 'the losses farmers are now sustaining'. He demonstrated that prices were one-third too low: he thought that wheat needed to be 96s a quarter in order to make a profit. Mr Ilott also reported that since 1815 'I can give the names of nearly fifty occupiers, who occupied to the amount of 24,000 acres, who have actually failed in this county, within my knowledge' and who have been reduced to pauperism or 'to a dependence on the benevolence of their friends, or to labour for their daily bread.'

# Fifehead Magdalen,
## *DORSET.*

TO BE

## *Sold by Auction,*

*By T. Lewis*

**ON MONDAY THE 27th DAY OF AUGUST, 1832,**

THE

# FARMING

## Of Mr. THOMAS GREEN,

*(Taken under a Distress for Rent,)*

COMPRISING

**ELEVEN** Prime Dairy Cows, Four Hog Heifers; about Sixty
Tons of excellent Meadow Hay, and sundry Dairy Utensils.

ALSO,

# THE FEED,

Till Christmas next, of between Thirty and Forty Acres of capital
Meadow Land.

THE Hay may be removed from off the Premises.

## SALE AT ONE O'CLOCK PRECISELY.

Thomas Green was a dairyman: typically for Dorset, he owned no land, only
grazing. Increased prosperity for larger farmers led to problems for
smaller ones: an improving landowner at Fifehead Magdalen made
a large fortune: Thomas Green went bankrupt.

During the eighteenth century farms had been getting larger, and the Napoleonic Wars accelerated this trend. Large farms swallowed up smaller ones, and in many cases became so large that they covered a whole parish. Holdings often covered 1,000-1,500 acres.

William Barnes' 'Eclogue: Two Farms in Woone' (1834) regrets the changes, recalling that there was now only one farm, where once there had been 'Eight farms avore they were a-drowed together'.

> An'now they don't imploy so many men
> Upon the land as work'd upon it then,
> Vor al they midden crop it worse, nor stock it.
> The lan'lord, to be sure, is into pocket

The landlord saved money because fewer farmhouses were needed – he could demolish those not wanted and save on repairs and Poor Rates. Amalgamation was also encouraged because landlords could charge higher rents for larger and more efficient farms.

The area under cultivation was also increased by 'improving' waste lands such as heaths, and by draining wet lands. Large farms employed less labour as they could afford machinery, and because (as Stevenson notes) on smaller farms 'every minute article of produce is carefully attended to'.

Labourers now had no chance of becoming farmers. William Barnes' 'Eclogue' continues:

> Aye, if a young chap, woonce, had any wit
> To try and screpe together some vew pound,
> To buy some cows an teke a bit o' ground
> He mid become a farmer, bit by bit.
> But hang it! Now the farms be all so big,
> An' bits o'ground so ske'ce, woone got no scope;
> If woone could seve a poun', woone coudden hope
> To keep noo live stock but a little pig.

The medieval open fields, where tenants held strips scattered all over the large fields, had gradually been superseded by enclosed farms with their land-holdings in a single block. The high prices during the Napoleonic Wars completed the process, with virtually all the remaining open fields being enclosed and cut up into farms. Thousands of acres were affected. The high cost of enclosure, which needed an Act of Parliament, tended to favour larger tenants who could afford it, so many small farmers were driven out by enclosure.

Labourers were also affected by the loss of common rights such as grazing for their animals, or collecting wood. A letter to *The Dorset County Chronicle* in January 1832 denies that the 'agricultural population' has been 'very much injured by Inclosure Acts. Everyone, who is conversant with rural affairs, knows that the condition and habits of labourers is much improved by an inclosure; that in a parish where there is any extent of waste [ie common] the population is in a greater state of destitution, more immoral and dishonest in their habits' than inclosed villages where 'lands are in a high state of cultivation' needing many labourers 'and where the eye of a master is constantly employed in superintending their comforts and checking disorderly habits. The borders of Commons are generally inhabited by poachers, smugglers and thieves'.

But this was an extreme view. William Barnes is much more sympathetic. 'In Eclogue: The Common A-Took in' (1834) two labourers mourn its loss. One is selling his geese, which he had kept on the common, and fears he will have to sell his cow as well. His losses are greater than merely his livestock:

> An'then, when I ha' nothen else to do,
> Why I can teke my hook an' gloves, an' goo
> To cut a lot o'f vuzz and briars
> Vor heten oevens, or vor lighten viers.
> An' when the children be too young to ern
> A penny, they can g'out in zunny weather,
> An' run about, an' get together
> A bag o' cow-dung vor to burn.

A scheme by Humphrey Repton to improve the landscape at Frome House, West Stafford, 1816. Many landowners wanted to adapt their grounds in fashionable styles in the early nineteenth century. This scheme (which was not carried out) is typical: the farm buildings are to be removed to open the view of the church, the river is dammed to form a lake and winding paths meander through the trees and bushes which replace the farmyard.

Even the right of labourers and their children to roam at will over the commons or open fields was objectionable to farmers and land-owners. One argument for the enclosure of Fordington Fields in 1813 was to remove the rights 'to wander over 3,000 acres of ground, committing trespass and depredations'.

The drive towards more capitalistic farming was reducing all the workers to the state of landless labourers, with a small area of ground

North Barn, Affpuddle, was built in 1802, and is one of seven built in that area early in the nineteenth century as part of the agricultural improvements. They all have brick bases to the cobb walls and huge thatched roofs.

to grow potatoes on if they were lucky. Their old rights of grazing, fuel gathering and simply access to land had kept them more independent: the landless labourer with no common rights was dependent on his employer for everything.

## GAME LAWS AND POACHERS

Shooting game was restricted to the upper classes: from the eigteenth century a licence was needed, and was only granted to gentlemen and their gamekeepers. Increasingly severe Game Laws from 1800 led to the penalty of transportation for poaching at night, even if the offender was not armed. Until 1827 landowners could legally set spring-guns (which were set off if anyone touched a wire) and man-traps to deter, maim or even kill poachers.

Dorset was a sporting county, as T. H. Williams describes in 1828: 'The principal part of the county is valuable for agricultural and pasturage, is covered with vast flocks of sheep, and it contains an abundance of game. From the open unenclosed state of its broad surface, it is more adapted for the various field sports of our wealthy and active gentry, then a county intersected by deep ravines, extensive woods, and mountain torrents, like Devonshire.'

With the enclosure of commons and the open fields, labourers lost their rights to take even rabbits from those areas. Shooting for the gentry and aristocracy meant less food and less freedom for the farm labourer and his family. Poaching still occurred, but was mostly carried out by gangs. In December 1822 Sir Robert Peel (then Secretary of State) was renting Lulworth Castle, and his gamekeeper was preparing for the visit of a shooting party. He heard that poachers were expected, and summoned twelve assistants. At midnight the poachers arrived, and when challenged they answered 'We are five and thirty strong, and are for Death or Glory: but we will not use fire-arms unless your party fire first'. A general fight ensured, both sides armed with clubs and swingels (like flails). The gamekeeper was injured, and the poachers retreated. Several of them were later captured, and four were transported to Australia.

The Game Laws were equally hard on tenant farmers. The landlord usually retained the shooting rights for himself, preventing any tenant from culling deer, rabbits and hares which damaged his crops.

Manor Farm, Gussage St Michael, is typical of simple Regency buildings, with its large windows which reach almost to the roof in the upper storey, shallow roof and fanlight over the main door. High prices for farm products in the early nineteenth century meant that farmers could well afford to rebuild their houses.

Compared with the advances which were to follow, Regency mechanisation seems insignificant, but in fact it had a huge effect on the labourers. Improvements in implements like harrows and rollers only slightly reduced the amount of work needed, but the new seed-drills and threshing machines were much more serious. Few threshing machines were used in Dorset until the 1820s because they were expensive and not always reliable, but by the time of the 1830s riots their use was widespread. William Barnes' 'Eclogue: Two Farms in Woone' (1834) laments their impact:

> *Why here wer vourteen men, zome years agoo,*
> *A-kept a-drashen half the winter drough;*
> *An' now, woone's drashels be'n't a bit 'o good.*
> *They got machines to drashy wi', plague teke em!*
> *I'd drash his busy zies vor'n if I could!*
> *Avore they took away our work, they ought*
> *To meke us up the bread our lebour bought.*

Threshing had been the main winter work for many labourers: beating the corn seed from the straw using a hinged stick (the flail) took a long time. Machines not only speeded the process: they made is possible to thresh fast to supply the market when prices were high.

John Pennie recorded the effects of these changes at Lulworth in a sarcastic letter of about 1810. He visited 'a plain, honest, but wealthy farmer óf the old school', a type he thought was becoming rare, and only surviving in 'some remote and obscure corner of the kingdom'. The farmer complains of his genteel children: 'Odd rott it, Suke here's the wold work going on: always humstrumming on thik there spindiddle thing [her prized grand piano] Buzz, buzz, like a bee in a tar-barrell . . . Why dostn't feed the poultry and the pigs, churn the cream, milk the cows and make the butter, and wear a cap on thy head as thy mother always used to do; not sit drest up here all the day".

He complains that his 'ould easy wooden arm-chair' once his grandfather's, has been burnt and he is supposed to sit on a 'fine

This early nineteenth century granary at Wyke Farm, Gillingham, is built on a timber frame set on stones supported (like mushrooms) to keep rats and mice from the corn stored in it. Most of the farm buildings constructed in the Regency have been demolished and replaced.

Waterloo Mill, Silton, must have been built in about 1815, the year of the battle. The corn mill (on the left) has stables and a cart-house attached, all with slated roofs. The cottage was built in a much more traditional style at the same date, with a thatched roof.

covered thing like a bed, which she [daughter] calls a sophy', and his great oak table has been banished to the kitchen. The children are only superficially genteel, insecure and only partly educated. The daughter (who calls her father Papa, to his great disgust) tells him that 'all respectable farmer's daughters dress like ladies nowadays; and I have been told, by those who know the world, that my edication has made me a fit match for any gentleman'.

A German Medical Officer serving in Weymouth from 1804-9 pronounced a similar verdict after spending such time with Dorset farmers; 'their sons and daughters spend their time in studying music and cultivating flower-gardens, quite heedless of the future, and desirous to emulate the ladies and gentlemen of the cities' (or indeed the local rural gentry).

William Barnes remembered being told the sad tale of a careful old farmer who was horrified by his brother (another farmer) whose daughters were going for lessons on the piano: 'Moosic and it be milken toime. Zummat will come o' that'. The something was bankruptcy and the farm was sold up. Whether this was entirely due to the daughters going to music lessons instead of milking the cows is not clear.

# THE LABOURERS

The agricultural labourers who made up the bulk of Dorset's population were poor in the late eighteenth century, but by 1830 they were desperate. Enclosure of the land, increasing population and falling prices for agricultural produces, all combined to make their wages lower. Since there were no factories, there was no alternative work for the labourers.

Sir Frederick Morton Eden surveyed the state of the poor in 1795 and took details of the 'domestic economy of a labourer's family' near Blandford. The man was 52, a widower with four children

The Town Mill, Gillingham, was partly rebuilt in the early nineteenth century and had typical slightly arched windows with small panes of glass. Gillingham mill was a cloth mill: manufacturing of a traditional sort survived in Dorset, but the massive industrialisation of the north never reached it.

under 8 and a daughter of 18 who managed the house. He was the only wage-earner, receiving 7s (35p) a week apart from harvest when he earnt 9s (45p) a week for 4 weeks. Bread and cheese three times a day was the constant diet, varied occasionally by potatoes mashed with fat taken from broth made with bullock's cheek. Treacle was used to sweeten the occasionally-drunk tea. Very little beer or milk was consumed.

The family would have been better fed in Blandford Workhouse, where Eden describes the diet as mostly bread and cheese, but with meat and vegetables twice a week. Bread he lists at 11d (5p) a quartern loaf (a huge loaf weighing about 4lb), but since the allowance of bread at the Workhouse was 1lb a day, even reckoning the children at half each, the family needed more than six loaves a week to equal the workhouse diet, and that would cost nearly a week's wages – 5s 6d from earnings of 7s. His rent was paid by the parish, but otherwise he received nothing from them. No wonder Eden records that 'for clothing for both himself and family, the man is principally indebted to his neighbours'.

Eden was not trying to select the very worst-off labourers, but this family was close to the bottom, only just surviving.

In 1815 Stevenson recorded the diet of the labourers:

> The food of the poor is wheaten bread, skim-milk cheese, puddings, potatoes, and other vegetables, with a small quantity of pickled pork and bacon. In some parts of the Vale of Blackmoor, the peasantry eat very little besides bread and skim-milk cheese, but labourers have, in some places at least, one or two pints of ale per day through the winter, and they sometimes hire a part of the fallows at 1s a perch, to plant with potatoes.

> About a bushel of wheat is consumed in a week by a man and his wife and three children, which is more than 10 bushels each per annum. Some people assert, that the above-mentioned quantity is enough to supply a family of six persons; and the poor are sometimes accursed of unnecessary wastefulness, in making cakes without yeast, and broiling or baking them on a gridiron, by which means, it is said, the quantity is lessened. Very little barley is used for bread.

Cottages built for labourers on the Marquis of Anglesey's estate at Bradford Abbas in 1825. Only the large estates were building model cottages like these for their labourers in the early nineteenth century.

In rural areas, women were more likely to be employed in cottage industries (like glove and button making) than men. Stevenson objects to their extravagance:

> Women are deemed too luxurious in drinking tea two or three times a day, instead of purchasing more substantial nourishment. The manufacture of shirt buttons, in some cases, appears to excite dissatisfaction among the farmers; they cannot get women to weed the corn for 9d. a day, when they can earn 12d or 18d. in button-making, which they lay out in fine clothes; and when they do come into the field, they are both awkward and unhealthy: they are also said to be unfit for service, and so ignorant as scarcely to know how to wash and mend their own clothes.

Women labourers making themselves so independent and unhousewifely that they were not suitable as servants strikes the Regency mind as very wicked. Having the double disadvantage of

Caroline Stephen, wife of the 3rd Earl of Ilchester, a
Grecian memorial at Melbury Sampford church. She died
in 1819, having been married seven years and leaving two sons
and two daughters. Such memorials reflect the vast gulf
between Dorset's gentry and the labourers on whom
many depended for a large share of their incomes.

being female and lower class should have kept them subser-
vient. The financial accounts given to the Select Committee of 1821
give the figures for the amount of manual labour needed for 100
acres of arable. Three regular men at 10s a week (one of them a
shepherd) and 2 boys at 3/6 a week are supplemented by extra labour
for weeding, hay-making, harvesting, threshing and winnowing. The
whole bill is only £182-17-6 per annum. Five horses were needed for
100 acres, and the food for each one is costed out at £25-7s, or 3s less
per annum than the total pay for a labourer, who also had to keep a
family. The £25 for each horse is just for its food and does not
include housing them. On his 10s a week a labourer had to pay rent.

John Scott, 1st Earl of Eldon (1751-1838) painted in 1828, at the end of his great career. He was born into the middle-class, trained as a lawyer, and was Lord Chancellor for 25 years. He purchased the Encombe estate in 1807 and was made an earl in 1821, both events marking his rise in the world. Like all the great landowners, much of his estate was let to tenant farmers, isolating him from the hardships and poverty endured by most farm workers.

In 1830 a letter in *The Dorset County Chronicle* discussed a London newspaper's estimated expenses for single able-bodied labourers. The letter covered 'the *minimum* quantity and quality of food necessary for the support of one able-bodied agricultural labourer in health and strength...'.

For a week, a peck of flour in bread or puddings, but most likely

| | |
|---|---|
| bread at 10d the quartern loaf | 3s 4d |
| 3½ lb of bacon at 9d per lb | 2s 7½d |
| 1 lb of butter at 1s per lb | 1s 0d |
| 1 lb of cheese at 8d per lb | 8d |
| 7 pots of beer at 3d, or an adequate quantity of milk | 1s 9d |
| Salt | 1d |

All this comes to 9s 5½d, or rather more than the 6s or 7s which the Dorset writer states was the usual wage in his area of Dorset, although sometimes supplemented by 1s 6d or 2s from the Poor Rates. He thought that the poor could buy bacon 2d or even 3d a lb cheaper than suggested, but even so when he visited thirty cottages of the poor and asked them if they had eaten bacon during the previous three weeks, half said they had had none, seven had eaten it five times and nine two or three. Very few of them could afford to keep pigs, and their general diet was bread and potatoes.

Lodgings, cooking and firing for a single man were estimated in the same report at 1s 6d a week, with shoes and clothing 2s 8d and washing 6d. This brought the total weekly expenses to 14s 1½d, or twice what many Dorset labourers had to support their families on.

The letter was published after the 1830 riots, and the author suggests that 'a little kind treatment, and a small increase of wages, from landlord or farmer, would silence all discontents, and prevent the labourers from joining in those associations, to which they are instigated no less by the arts of designing men, than by the real and substantial evils by which they are oppressed'. The man who wrote the letter thought himself sympathetic to the labourers, and had 'no slight acquaintance with the feelings and conditions of the poor', but still he could not see that it was wrong for labourers to be paid wages so low that they could not feed themselves and their families.

## THE RIOTS OF 1830

Trouble started first in Kent in the autumn. The hated threshing machines were destroyed and ricks set on fire by bands of labourers. In late November it spread to Dorset, and *The Dorset County Chronicle* of 2nd December had to admit 'that great distress has been, and is prevalent amongst the agricultural population . . . but no distress, however great, can palliate that destruction of property which has taken place'.

The labourers were demanding higher wages, and the abolition of threshing machines. Threatening letters, usually signed by the imaginary leader of the riots, Captain Swing, were sent to farmers. A typical group was one from Pulham, 'a party of labourers, about 50

Upwey in 1818, a rich farming landscape with a milkmaid in the foreground.
Rows of neat thatched cottages housed the farm labourers, while the bigger
houses are either farmhouses or the villas of the new middle class. An
apparently calm and contented landscape; but in reality there were many
tensions beneath the surface.

or 60 in number', who destroyed a draining-machine (all machines
were suspect because they took away work). 'At the same time they
demanded money, and succeeded in obtaining about seven pounds'.
They moved on to one of the big houses 'where they renewed their
demands; but a gentleman who was in the house refused compliance,
and by his firmness and the assistance of the domestics . . . was
enabled to deter them from committing any outrage' (*The Dorset
County Chronicle*).

Mrs Floyer of West Stafford was much admired for her firm
handling of the labourers who came to her house to demand higher
wages. She said 'I shall do no such thing – go along – not one penny.

My purse has always been open to your sick families, and I shall not raise your wages'.

The upper and middle classes responded very quickly to the threats. 'An alarm was given in Blandford, that a party of rioters were in the neighbourhood, destroying machinery and other property; in consequence of which about 250 of the principal gentlemen, trades-men and farmers ... were mounted and armed'. The armed posse sounds rather like a hunt: they beat through several villages until they caught up with the rioters at Sixpenny Handley, 'where after some exertion they succeeded in capturing several of the ringleaders of the gang who had been active in burning and destroying the machines.

'In the different villages the patrol passed through, they assured the labourers that their case should be taken into the most serious con-sideration, and that their wages should be increased; on which they expressed their readiness to stand by the gentry and farmers to the last, should any of the dissaffected bands appear in the neighbour-hood'.

No-one seems to have any real intention of increasing the labourers' pathetic wages, except Mr Portman of Bryanston who had 'agreed to raise wages to 10s a week ...' and had also undertaken to reduce the rents farmers paid him for land.

Big houses in the north of the county were in a state of siege. 'A band of machine-breakers who had just met with a warm reception and gathered together at West Park, was expected to pay a visit to Cranborne. The Marquis of Salisbury promptly took up his head-quarters at the Manor House where, in concert with the Magistrates, Clergy and Gentry of the district, measures were arranged for our protection. The Old Hall was converted into a Barrack room, where a guard of yeoman was daily stationed during a fortnight with steeds caparisoned and fully equipped for a sally at a moment's notice'.

A midnight alarm that the rioters were going to pillage Cranborne 'and put the inhabitants to the sword' turned out to be a 'cruel hoax', However, 'Intelligence was received that the machine breakers were actually engaged in their nefarious business at Chapel Farm, near Handley. Forty chosen horsemen with Lord Salisbury at their head, together with a body of special constables on foot, hastened to

the scene, where after silently witnessing the savage work of destr-
tion, and holding a parley with the rioters, they quietly dispersed –
greatly to the satisfaction of many, whose courage had begun to ooze
out of their finger-ends'. (This seems to be an eye-witness account,
noted in the back of a copy of *Chronicles of Cranborne Chase* (1841),
in the Dorset County Museum.

The rioters also set fire to hay, corn and reed ricks, and in extreme
cases, barns. At Bradle, near Corfe Castle, a large barn was set afire,
and the Wareham fire engine was dispatched. 'So rapid had been the
work of destruction' that before the engine arrived the barn, the corn
stored in it and a reed stack of more than a thousand sheaves was
destroyed. Several gypsies, encamped nearby, 'were apprehended the
same night', but despite thorough cross-examination of these usual
rural bogeymen, it could not be proved that they had lit the fire (*The
Dorset County Chronicle.*)

Mary Frampton described James Frampton leading about 150
mounted farmers, enrolled as special constables, towards Winfrith
where rioters were gathering. They found 'the mob, urged on from
behind hedges, etc., by a number of women and children'. The men
were respectful, and advanced 'with their hats in their hands, to
demand increase of wages, but would not listen to the request that
they should disperse. The Riot Act was read. They still surged
forward, and came close to Mr Frampton's horse. He then collared
one man, but in giving him in charge he slipped from his captors by
leaving his smock frock in their hands'. Eventually three 'ringleaders' were arrested. The mob was described as 'being in general
very fine-looking young men, and particularly well-dressed, as if they
had put on their best clothes.'

The disturbances only lasted a fortnight, and seventy-one prisoners
were tried at a special court in Dorchester in January 1831, charged
with burning threshing machines and rioting. 15 were acquitted, 12
sentenced to transportation and the others imprisoned for 18 months
or less.

The local paper, in an editorial, reflects the fears the riots
produced. 'Considerable dread has been expressed that the elements
of anarchy have merely subsided for a time, and that another
explosion of a still more devastating character will break forth, and

terminate but in a revolution'. The French Revolution of forty years earlier was much in men's' minds: a further upheaval there had just removed Charles X from the throne, and several other countries (including Belgium and Poland) were in the throes of revolution that very autumn.

D.O.P. Okeden, a landowner and magistrate, had been closely involved with the suppression of the riots and in regular contact with central government. In early December, only just after the riots, he published a public letter to the Dorset MPs 'on the subject of Poor-relief and Labourers' Wages'. He had a very straightforward view: 'if they who have to work to bestow will not pay for the health, youth, and strength expended on its execution, then such employers must be prepared to meet a legal demand for the maintenance of the workman in sickness, age or infirmity; or to behold him starved to death; or to encounter the violence of man reduced by hunger and want to desperation'. He quoted the Bible to complete his argument: 'the Labourer is worthy of his hire'.

Even Okeden did not think that the labourer could be independent: 'the Poor must be left very much to the care and kindness of their more wealthy and natural Protectors. The resident Landowner, the Clergyman of the Parish, and let me add the Farmer, all stand in this responsible situation. The Poor must live, to use their own forcible and homely expression, "from hand to mouth"'. The poor and the labourers are interchangeable terms.

SELF-HELP

Friendly Societies of labourers had been established in Dorset from the mid-eighteenth century, but by 1794 there were only twelve. The hard times after the Napoleonic wars increased the number to 137 in 1819, and another 59 were formed between 1820 and 1834. Clearly, only a small proportion of Dorset labourers belonged to such a society.

The Articles of Symondsbury Friendly Society (1836) are typical and explain the system. The purpose of the Society 'is to raise a fund by subscription and donation for the mutual relief and maintenance of the Members thereof in sickness &c. Each member is to pay two

Jug made (probably in Staffordshire) for the Wimborne St Giles Friendly Society, probably 1830s. It would have been used for beer at the meetings of the Society. Its light-hearted decoration seems inappropriate considering the problems of the labourer members.

shillings and sixpence' for entry money, 'to be in perfect health previous to his admission, to reside within three miles of Symondsbury Church', to be aged between 15 and 50, and to be approved by the majority of the members. When the man had been a member for 18 months, he could claim 5s a week sick money for the first month, and three shillings a week for the rest of his illness. The Society also supplied a doctor. At the death of a member, the others were to subscribe one shilling each towards his funeral. The 'general yearly meeting' of the Society was a celebration: the members marched to church, and after the ceremony held a dinner.

The Symondsbury rules show that, like many such Societies, it was only established for a limited period – seven years in this case. After that time the monies would be shared between the surviving members, each share less what each man had been paid in sickness benefit. The twenty-five rules were printed in a booklet which was given to each new member, and the final page is endorsed by a barrister who certifies that the rules conform with current laws. The

Symondsbury labourers were being very careful to make it clear that their Society was legal. The list of honorary members (who did not receive benefits) on the front of the rules includes three local clergymen and ten other who were farmers or landowners, confirming the acceptable nature of the society.

William Cobbett called these Societies 'making the Pauper help the Pauper'. Many societies were so small that paying for an epidemic would have wiped them out financially. They were also vulnerable to fraud: stewards sometimes ran off with all the money. A larger Dorset Friendly Society might have helped, but attempts to set one up in 1826 failed.

MECHANIC'S INSTITUTE. Although they were mainly an urban phenomena, Mechanic's Institutes could have helped labourers. Some were involved with the early Trades Unions, and indeed the Plymouth Mechanic's Institute held the celebration of the return home of the Tolpuddle Martyrs in 1838.

Bridport was the earliest Dorset Institute, founded in December 1830, just after the riots. It is clear that it was intended for the lower classes of the town, not the agricultural labourers, and it indeed was to play no part in the struggles of the Tolpuddle Martyrs.

THE LABOURER'S FRIEND SOCIETY. In 1832 a meeting at Sturminster Newton voted to establish a Dorset branch of the national Labourers' Friend Society, which existed to provide large allotments at reasonable rents so that labourers could grow part of their own food. The speakers referred to the then current practice of Dorset farmers in letting land to the poor at £9 an acre, when the farmers were only paying 35/- rent an acre for the same land. The Society wanted landowners to let land directly to the poor, and to keep it manured. Some Dorset landowners were already doing this. For example, Lord Anglesey had 'recently erected ten most commodious, and even ornamental cottages, for the use and benefit of ten married men of *approved good character*; with a quarter of an acre of good land attached to each' at Stalbridge.

The Rev. Walter of Hazelbury Bryan had accommodated 22 people on 8 acres and insisted 'upon every one of the little tenants going to some place of worship on the Lord's Day – and that a first or second conviction for drunkenness' should be enough to evict a tenant. Walter was more liberal than might be expected: he did not insist that tenants attend the parish church, thus admitting dissenters as tenants.

The Literary & Scientific Institute, Bridport, originally the Bridport Mechanic's Institute. The fine classical building was erected about 1834, and is surprisingly large and imposing considering that such Institutes had only existed for ten years. Bridport was one of the earliest in the whole county, being founded in 1831. They were intended for the education and improvement of the working classes, but many soon became more middle-class and were renamed. The building was paid for by the local MP.

William Barnes' poem 'Eclogue: the 'Lotments', published in 1834, extolled the allotment system:

> JOHN
> *I wish the girt woones had a-got the greace*
> *To let out land lik' this in ouer pleace;*
> *But I do fear there'll never be nwone vor us,*
> *An' I can't tell whatever we shall do:*
> *We be a most a-starven, an' we'd goo*
> *To 'merica, if we'd enough to car us.*
>
> RICHARD
> *Why 'twer the squire, good now! A worthy man,*
> *That vu'st brought into ouer pleace the plan;*
> *He zaid he'd let a vew odd eacres*
> *O'land to us poor leab'ren men;*
> *An faith, he had enough o'teakers*

The allotments were certainly useful, but unlike the earlier commons they were not a right, but a charity. The labourers had to be deserving in order to rent them. The Labourers' Friend Society by-passed the farmers, letting land directly from the land-owner to the labourer, so at least workers could keep their allotments if they changed farms. The movement spread fast, and in a few years 70% of Dorset labourers had such plots.

# CHURCH AND CHAPEL

In 1800 the Church of England was still the established church with enormous power and influence. In order to serve in public life, be elected as an MP, serve as an officer in the Army, or even go to Oxford or Cambridge (the only universities) a person had to belong to the Church of England (i.e. be Anglican). Catholics and all non-conformists were excluded. The Church of England was thus the State church, but with the enormous growth of non-conformacy (particularly Methodism) pressure for reform increased. The landed

Holy Trinity Church, Dorchester, was rebuilt in 1823 in a typical Regency type of medieval: very unconvincing. Typically, Holy Trinity had painted rather than stained glass in its east windows, and the little turrets at the west end look more like chimneys. This church was demolished in 1875 and replaced by a much duller, but more 'medieval' one.

Charles Weld, from the Lulworth landowning family, was made
the first British Cardinal since the sixteenth century in 1829.
Some even thought he might be made Pope.
Generally Catholics were feared because it was thought that
their loyalty to the church made them too international,
and possibly disloyal.

gentry of Dorset (and elsewhere) were thoroughly Anglican, with
support for Methodism and other non-conformist sects coming from
the lower orders.

A poster produced as a protest about demolishing the tower of
Holy Trinity church, Dorchester, in 1823 complained about depriv-
ing the town of its only public clock, but the most important reason
for preservation was that 'the removal of the Tower would destroy
all the appearance of an ESTABLISHED NATIONAL CHURCH'.
The tower demonstrated that the Church was part of the Church of
England, and therefore part of the reigning establishment.

Pressure to remove the restrictions on both non-conformists and
Catholics was intense. Restrictions were eased from 1812 for Protes-
tant non-conformists and removed virtually entirely in 1828. The

Allington church, built in 1827, shows the neat classical style popular then. It could be mistaken for a non-conformist chapel. The inside is even simpler, just a large hall filled with pews, altar rails flanked by twin pulpits and carefully arranged curtains around the east window. Most of Allington was destroyed by fire in 1796, which is why so much of it is early nineteenth century.

The Rectory, Winterborne Came, is deliberately picturesque, with verandahs and complicated glazing in all the windows. It was built early in the nineteenth century, and was the home of William Barnes from 1862-1886. The verandahs made the house so dark that 'windows' were cut into them in the twentieth century.

following year Catholics gained the same freedoms.

Religious tolerance was unusual, but it did exist. Mr Charles Bowles (later agent for Lord Grovesnor at Shaftesbury) speaking after the Dorset County election in March 1823 said that his idea of religious liberty was that everyone should worship God in his own way, should accept that others had different ways, and 'that every person who contributes to the exigencies of the state, whether Jew, Turk, Mahometan, Deist, or Christian [with the exception of non-natives] should be entitled to have a share in the government of the country'. The Catholic peers were currently banned from the House of Lords, and, if they were admitted, 'it is possible that they may meet with worse company than they have been in before'. (*Western Flying Post*)

The Church of England in Regency times was seen by the reforming

St James Church, Poole, of 1820. The pillars are of timber, four huge posts, like masts, and the capitals and ceiling are plaster. The Victorians disapproved of these light-hearted Regency churches, with their incorrect materials. There is no difference between this view and the same view inside a big, prosperous non-conformist chapel of the same date.

Victorians as being at a low ebb, but the situation was more varied than the reformers claimed. Mrs L. C. Boswell-Stone, writing in the late 1880s, remembered the Rev Nat Templeman, a vicar of Dorchester who died in 1813. 'From all I have heard he would at the present day be regarded as very dark, even for the dusky church times in which he lived. But I confess to a weakness for the old parsons ... familiar guests, always welcome, entering into our joys and sorrows, knowing everybody in the parish; no need to find them out, because, if people wanted help, the first to be thought of was the clergyman, whether the want was spiritual or temporal'. Mrs Stone had lived through the Victorian church reforms, and so had a good perspective.

Worldly some of the clergymen certainly were, and mercenary considerations were sometimes prominent. A squabble over a clergyman who had been offered the rich living at Long Crichel as a temporary measure until the son of the owner of the living was old enough to take it, and who then refused to leave when asked to do so, is reported in horror by Hutchins (1813). As a result many 'who had intended to educate their children in the clerical profession, have turned their thoughts to another way of life'.

Ministers in the Church of England were not paid a uniform salary: historical accidents had left some livings very rich, and many very poor. Pluralism (the holding of two or more livings together) was common, and some clergymen didn't live in their parish, instead employing a lowly curate to do the work on their behalf.

Some clergy helped their poor parishioners, but in general they were very much part of the establishment. During the agricultural riots of 1830 the local paper solemnly reported that 'a clergyman of this county anxious to prevent the contagion of disaffection spreading amongst his parishioners' sent for a parcel of tracts from the Society for Promoting Christian Knowledge. 200 copies of the *Homily against Disobedience and Wilful Rebellion* and 200 copies of *Miller's Thoughts for Labouring Classes* were dispatched. At least the starving labourers did not have to pay to be told that they should do as their betters told them – the copies were 'for gratuitous distribution'.

It is difficult to know what proportion of people went to church, but it was certainly fewer than in Victorian times. Estimates suggest only one-third of the adult population attended church, and many fewer actually took communication, which was only celebrated about four times a year.

A German Medical Officer quartered at Weymouth in 1805 was not impressed by English religious celebrations:

The festival of Easter is observed in England, as, indeed, are all

St Mary's church in the centre of Weymouth, built 1815-1817. It has a neo-classical front to the street and a little turret, and is all of Portland stone.

other religious festivals, as a time more particularly set apart for rioting and drinking. The higher orders of society, in fact, do not observe them at all; and this difference appears, at first, exceedingly strange to the continental visitor. On the Easter Monday of this year an event occurred in our neighbourhood which dashed the mirth of the populace; for, in one of these drunken revels, a dragoon met his death in an affray with a sailor.

The simple faith and rituals of Abbotsbury fishermen are a great contrast:

'Before the first launching of the boat in every week, when the net and all are ready, the captain says, "Let us pray!", when the whole crew, bare-headed, fall on their knees, around the boat, and join in silent address to the Almighty, recommending themselves and their undertakings to his protection and favour'. Afterwards 'they rise, and all saying "in the name of God", their united efforts thrust the boat from the shore'. A similar ceremony, but with rather more selfish overtones, took place at the weekly meeting to divide the takings. All the men from the boat then knelt around table and thanked heaven for its favours, adding "The God who gave us this, can give us more!'" (*Hutchins*)

The Rev Henry Moule was made vicar of Fordington, just outside Dorchester in 1829. He was one of the new evangelical vicars, and caused much dissension in the parish. When he asked for water to be put into the font for a christening, it was explained to him that it was not necessary, as the old parson used to manage by spitting on his hand. Some, when taking communion, had held up the communion cup and said 'Here's the good health of our Lord Jesus Christ', and women had been paid to take communion so as to keep the numbers up. Moule was described as a Methodist (a term of abuse amongst Anglicans) and he and his children hooted at in the streets.

Social divisions were preserved even in church: Robert Southey, the poet, writing in 1808 and pretending to be a Spanish visitor, noted in Dorset, 'They have an abominable custom of partitioning their churches into divisions which they call pews, and which are private property; so that the wealthy sit at their ease, or kneel upon cushions, while the poor stand during the whole services'.

## NON-CONFORMISTS

Baptists, Congregationalists, Unitarians, Quakers and other sects had existed in Dorset from the seventeenth century, but it was the new Methodism which swept the county in the early nineteenth century. Methodism as a separate church only existed from 1795, but established itself so quickly that by 1840 it was the most important sect outside the Anglican church.

In 1805, Methodist preachers in Dorset were described as a 'select band of local preachers, whose delight it was, on Sabbath days to itinerate through the county, quelling the rage of rustic revilers with the magic story of the Cross'. These early Methodists suffered much opposition: at Owermoigne many labourers joined the Methodists early in the century and 'this hallowed excitement produced much wonder amongst the squirearchy of the neighbourhood: and one of

The Unitarian Chapel in Wareham is all stucco-brick rendered
to look like stone. It opened in 1830.

their number showed his resentment by turning the Methodists out
of their little cottages into the road'. The middle and upper classes
often objected to early Methodist preachers: at Burton Bradstock in
1811 a Methodist minister 'attempted to preach in the open air,
but was compelled to desist, by the united efforts of an admiral, a
magistrate, a clergyman, a churchwarden and a constable', which the
Methodist historian saw as 'a good opportunity to convey a little
wholesome doctrine to the upper classes'. The lower classes were not
much better: at Bridport 'the rabble and a few lewd fellows of the
baser sort assailed [the minister and his congregation]. Dead rats,
various kinds of filth, and stones were thrown, and on one occasion
'an innkeeper heated some small copper coins and then, to create
a disturbance, amuse the mob, and burn the fingers of the boys,

scattered them amongst the crowd'. (*Methodism in Dorset* 1870).

Methodism was based on personal salvation, and in its earlier years was democratic. The congregation, and lay preachers (like George Loveless, one of the Tolpuddle Martyrs) were as important as the ministers, so that ordinary labourers could both participate more fully in services and be a real part of the church government. Both were impossible in the Church of England. Methodists were more independent from the upper classes than Anglicans, and the local Methodist organisations helped with education. However, Methodism preached acceptance of the existing social order, along with submissiveness and obedience. Very few Union or Chartist men were Methodist: George Loveless and others of the Tolpuddle Martyrs were exceptions. Generally it was a stabilising influence: Methodists were known for their thrift, industry and sobriety.

George Loveless was a Methodist lay preacher, and his writings show the anger of the ordinary labourer towards the Anglican church. In 1838 he published a pamphlet called *The Church Shown Up*, attacking the Church of England as being part of government rather than about God. 'Was religion first established in grandeur and all the pomp of state? Did it require the smiles of the great, the wisdom of the learned, or the wealth of the mighty to make it spread and grow?' Loveless answers from the Bible that it was not, and that the disciples were simple poor fishermen. He reports a sermon in a local church where the minister claimed that 'Roman Catholics and the different bodies of Dissenters were joining with the infidels to trample on the Bible and trying to overturn the Church'. Loveless thought it 'criminal to persecute any man for conscience sake, and that although men differed in religious opinion he did not see why that should make them worse citizens, or less loyal and dutiful subjects'.

Most Regency churches were medieval, and were in poor condition, damp and often very dark. The ideal for churches then was very different, as shown in the few completely new ones which were light with large windows, rather plain and whitewashed. Even the new churches had galleries across the back and down the sides to provide more seating. One gallery was normally used by the singers and instrumentalists. The rest of the church was filled with high pews, mostly privately owned. Many pretty neo-classical wall memorials were put up at this time, and a few churches added painted glass to their windows.

## SCHOOLS

Schools reflect all the features of the age. They were seen as needing reforming, and were the cause of much strife between the Church of England and the non-conformists. For the first time in 1834, grants were available from central government for schools, and so the period marks the true beginning of our modern educational system.

In the eighteenth century there had been dame schools for younger children, and the old-established town grammar schools for boys. From the 1790s Sunday Schools for general education were established, and the church and chapels started to become involved with the education of children.

THE CHURCH OF ENGLAND SCHOOLS. The National Society for Promoting the Education of the Poor in the Principles of the Established Church (thankfully usually known as the National Society) established schools in Dorset from 1812, and worked towards providing a school for each larger parish or group of smaller ones. By 1822 they were running 152 schools in the county, with over nine thousand pupils, some of whom attended Sundays or evenings rather than during the day.

In their 1813 Report they estimated that 160 schools would be needed and hoped that 'the period is not very distant, when every child, residing in the most obscure hamlet in the County, will have the advantage of this system of religious education'. Reading, writing and arithmetic were taught along with religion. Pupils only attended for a few years, and were mostly under the age of eleven.

The system of education used was that invented by Dr Bell, Vicar of Swanage (1801-9) in India in the late eighteenth century. His Madras system meant that one teacher could manage a whole school: the master instructed the monitors, who then instructed the pupils.

Even this new education differed for the two sexes. A girl's school

The British School in Poole, photographed in the later nineteenth century. It was probably built in the 1830s: these early schools rarely survive because they proved to be too small. The interior is the upper room, one big hall. The chairs were probably for the monitors, with the benches around them for the pupils. The school has been demolished.

was established in Dorchester in 1813, and half the day was to be spent on knitting, sewing and mending. 'No girl to be permitted to learn to write or cypher [maths], till she has completed her ninth year, nor then, unless she can read in the Bible fluently, repeat the Catechism, Prayers, knit stockings and do all sorts of common plain work'. (Many of us would never have learnt to write with those needlework requirements).

The stress was on Religion. The rules for East Stoke Schools of about 1838 state that the pupils 'must try to be better children for what they learn, if they would be happy when they die' and that 'they must remember that when on earth, they are training to live with God for ever in heaven'.

Sunday schools taught reading and writing as well as religion, alongside cleanliness and respect for one's betters. At Marnhull, only six months after the Sunday School was established in 1824, 'the cleanly appearance and good behaviour of the children truly evinced the benefit resulting from such an institution'. (*Sherborne Mercury*).

NON-CONFORMIST SCHOOLS. Virtually everyone would have agreed with the need for education to be religious, there was disagreement as to the exact form of that religion. There were too many non-conformist sects for it to be easy for them to establish schools, and even the largest (the Methodists) were too poor and lacked the central organisation necessary to run a country-wide schools system. The British and Foreign Society was the closest to non-conformacy as it took a broad Christian approach, avoiding sectarianism. Even by 1846, there were only twelve British Schools in Dorset, all of them in towns.

Methodism was, however, an important factor in education, through its Sunday and evening schools, and perhaps even more through its belief in the capacity of the labourers to learn. Many, like George Loveless, educated themselves within Methodism, and like him, became preachers.

# THE POOR LAW AND THE
# WORKHOUSE

From Elizabethan times the parish had taken responsibility for its own sick and aged, sometimes even building a poor-house where they could be accommodated. The money came from a local Poor Rate, assessed on property. With rising prices in the Napoleonic Wars, the system was extended so that the parish supplemented the inadequate wages of labourers. The parish made up a family's income on a scale relating to the price of a loaf of bread and the number in the family. Even with the extra from the Poor Rate, wages were only barely sufficient for survival.

The costs of the poor to the parish grew enormously over the period. At Portland in 1801 £282 was expended, but by 1814 the annual expenditure was £693. Parishes organised celebrations as well as administering the Poor Laws. At Cerne Abbas the peace of 1814 was properly celebrated: 'About Four Hundred Poor Men, Women, and Children of the Town were regaled with a plentiful Dinner of Beef, Plum-pudding and other warm provision, served upon a range of tables in length 255 feet, in the centre of Abbey Street terminated at *each* extremity by a triumphal Arch, decorated with Flowers and Laurels and a Hogshead of good Strong Beer'. It all cost £50 'provided by voluntary subscriptions' (Churchwardens' Accounts Book).

In the 1820s the parish system was extended further. The Select Committee on Labourers' Wages in 1823 heard evidence from Rev. Henry Walter, who had recently moved to Dorset from Lincolnshire. He had been horrified by methods used in his village at Hazelbury Bryan. 'A farmer wishing to have any job done on his farm, sent to the overseers, and said, "I want two, three, four, or five men, whom you will place upon your books"'. The overseer of the Poor was actually employing the labourers, and then sending them out to work for farmers. Tradesmen, who paid part of the Poor Rate, could not take advantage of this, and labourers who owned any property at all could not receive money from the Overseer and so had no work. Walter had been told that these labourers with a little land were some of the best workmen, but none had had any work for six months because the farmers said 'we cannot take you since we can get others for nothing'. In fact, as Walter admitted, the principal payers of the Poor Rate were the self-same farmers. Wages were 1od or 1s a day.

The Dorset magistrate and landowner, D.O.P. Okeden, writing in 1830, just after the riots, defined the inadequacies and stupidities of the system:

'The Labourer who worked for "A" is repeatedly paid the balance due to him for his labour by "B", and vice versa; and so proceeds the system, until the whole legalized payment becomes a sort of methodical lottery, a scramble, in which however, the Labourer never fails to obtain his deferred balance from some one or other of his employers; or perhaps from one who never employed him at all, and never till the moment of application ever heard of his existence.'

Oakdon states that one-sixth of the monies collected for the Poor Rates was spent on sorting out who was entitled to it, and disliked the whole system: the payers 'gave without charity' and the labourers 'received without gratitude.'

Okedon thought the labourer should be paid 'full and fair wages. Instead, however, of raising Wages to their only equitable level, an arrangement has pervaded almost all England, (I fear it has been too prevalent in Dorsetshire), by which the Wages are systematically depressed, and the Poor Rates proportionately raised. It has been the custom of whole districts to settle the Labourer's wages at a most inadequate sum, and to make up his necessary subsistance from the Poor Book. A more unjust, a more impolitic, and more illegal, a more destructive measure never was devised'. The 'settlement' which caused so much dispute and expense was the right of a person to claim support from the parish. Paupers had to prove they had 'settlement' (i.e. belonged to the parish), to get poor relief.

By the 1820s the parish system was seen as inefficient and needing reform. The Poor Law Amendment Act of 1834 made new Boards of Guardians responsible for the poor. They responded to directives from Commissioners in London, and were an elected body. The numbers eligible to vote were not huge, but the change was great, and pointed towards a modern system of government.

Dorset was divided into twelve unions of parishes, each with a Board of Guardians. Each of them quickly built a Workhouse on the model of the seventeenth century House of Relief and Correction: the name indicate the attitudes. Some towns, like Dorchester, already had a workhouse. These were abolished, and the inmates were moved to the new Union Workhouses.

It was intended that life in the Workhouse should be harder than life outside, to deter able-bodied paupers from entering. It was impossible to give Workhouse inhabitants less food than many of them had had outside: they would have starved to death. William Barnes' Eclogue of 1834 on 'The New Poor Laws' has two labourers talking about the food: 'An 'tis but scanty prog tha'l gie within/The house; 't'll kip em plaguy thin'. But the worst aspect for them is the separation of man and wife:

> Aye, they be guain, ya know, to kip asunder
> The menvolk in the poorhouse, vrom their wives.
> How wull the women like thick plan I wonder?
> How wull the menvolk like to liead such lives?
> They mid as well, I think, each wi' his bride
> Goo back to Church an' have ther knot untied.

Under the earlier system, labourers who could not get work were given money and allowed to remain in their homes. Under the new system they had to leave their cottage – even their village – and live in a workhouse far from home. The Workhouse was intended to put labourers off claiming relief, and it succeeded.

*The Dorset County Chronicle* (22 May 1834) declared that 'the principles upon which' the new Poor Law was founded were 'heartless and utterly opposed to the better feelings of human nature'. Its

Beaminster Union Workhouse, photographed in 1910. The central part was built in 1838 and looks like a classical country house. In fact it was from one of the standard designs for workhouses. Beaminster Union consisted of 26 parishes, centered on the workhouse at Stoke Water, just outside Beaminster.

operation will be to draw a more distinct line of demarcation between rich and poor than has ever before existed, even in the days of feudal pomp and tyranny.' In the workhouses 'the poor will be set apart like wild beasts in a cage, staked off from their fellow-men, and regarded as beings of a different caste'. The conservative *Chronicle* also disliked 'the extraordinary powers proposed to be vested in the Commissioners'.

The Union and its workhouse was established as the main means of poor relief, although some money was still given to the poor who stayed in their own cottages. The workhouse continued as an object of hatred into the twentieth century.

# THE TOLPUDDLE MARTYRS

The problems of the agricultural labourers culminated in attempts to form Unions. In 1833 a tiny Friendly Society was formed in Tolpuddle amongst the farm labourers. Two years earlier they had made an agreement with the farmers for 9s a week wages. Subsequently the farmers reduced the wage to 8s a week, and then to 7s. The Society was formed because 'it was impossible to live honestly on such scanty means'. The farmers were about the lower the wages again, to 6s a week. The labourers took advice from London Trades Unions because Unions had only been legal since 1824. There were perhaps a dozen men who joined the Tolpuddle Friendly Society, most of them Methodists.

Members of the Tolpuddle union went through an odd and deeply serious initiation rite: all early Trades Unions did this. At Tolpuddle the initiates were blindfolded, 'words from the Bible' read to them, and when the blindfold was removed they were looking at a two metre high painting of Death as a skeleton with his scythe in his hand. 'Remember thine end' was chanted three times. Afterwards an oath binding the members together was taken, which is why they were prosecuted.

In February 1834 local magistrates had placards posted in Dorset, stating that Trades Unions were illegal, because members swore a secret oath. The Magistrates were applying an obscure law which had only been passed to deal with mutiny in the navy in the 1790s. Union supporters made fun of the upper-class Freemasons who 'set the people the example of this foolish mummery, and this improper oath-taking . . . Now, we are constantly told that the great use of gentlemen is to set a bright and shining example to the poor' and all the Unions had done was to follow the gentlemen's example.

All six of the Tolpuddle members were arrested – George and James Loveless (brothers); Thomas and John Standfield (father and

# CAUTION.

WHEREAS it has been represented to us from several quarters, that mischievous and designing Persons have been for some time past, endeavouring to induce, and have induced, many Labourers in various Parishes in this County, to attend Meetings, and to enter into Illegal Societies or Unions, to which they bind themselves by unlawful oaths, administered secretly by Persons concealed, who artfully deceive the ignorant and unwary,—WE, the undersigned Justices think it our duty to give this Public Notice and Caution, that all Persons may know the danger they incur by entering into such Societies.

ANY PERSON who shall become a Member of such a Society, or take any Oath, or assent to any Test or Declaration not authorized by Law ---

Any Person who shall administer, or be present at, or consenting to the administering or taking any Unlawful Oath, or who shall cause such Oath to be administered, although not actually present at the time ---

Any Person who shall not reveal or discover any illegal Oath which may have been administered, although not actually present at the time ---

Any Person who shall not reveal or discover any illegal Oath which may have been administered, or any illegal Act done or to be done ---

Any Person who shall induce, or endeavour to persuade any other Person to become a Member of such Societies, WILL BECOME

## *Guilty of Felony,*
### and be liable to be
## TRANSPORTED FOR SEVEN YEARS.

ANY PERSON who shall be compelled to take such an Oath, unless he shall declare the same within four days, together with the whole of what he shall know touching the same, will be liable to the same Penalty.

Any Person who shall directly or indirectly maintain correspondence or intercourse with such Society, will be deemed Guilty of an Unlawful Combination and Confederacy, and on Conviction before one Justice, on the oath of one Witness, be liable to a Penalty of TWENTY POUNDS, or to be committed to the Common Gaol or House of Correction, for THREE CALENDAR MONTHS; or if proceeded against by Indictment, may be CONVICTED OF FELONY, and be TRANSPORTED FOR SEVEN YEARS.

Any Person who shall knowingly permit any Meeting of any such Society to be held in any House, Building, or other Place, shall for the first offence be liable to the Penalty of FIVE POUNDS; and for every other offence committed after Conviction, be deemed Guilty of such Unlawful Combination and Confederacy, and on Conviction before one Justice, on the oath of one Witness, be liable to a Penalty of TWENTY POUNDS, or to Commitment to the Common Goal or House of Correction, FOR THREE CALENDAR MONTHS; or if proceeded against by Indictment may be

## Convicted of Felony, and Transported for SEVEN YEARS.

COUNTY OF DORSET,
WAREHAM DIVISION.

February 20th, 1834.

JOHN BOND.
JOHN H. CALCRAFT.
JAMES C. FYLER.
GEORGE PICKARD, Junior.
NATHANIEL BOND.

C. Groves, Printer, Wareham.

The poster which was displayed all over Dorset in February 1834, declaring that Union oaths were illegal. The Tolpuddle Martyrs were prosecuted for such an illegal oath.

son); James Hammett and James Brine. Two other members of the Friendly Society gave evidence against the six men, who were found guilty and sentenced to seven year's transportation to Australia.

George Loveless, their leader and the most articulate member, handed an address to the judge in court after being found guilty: 'My Lord, if we have violated any law, it was not done intentionally: we have injured no man's reputation, character, person or property: we were uniting together to preserve ourselves, our wives, and our children, from utter degradation and starvation'. The judge mumbled over this statement so that the jury could not hear or understand it. The magistrates would have done much better to have selected labourers who were not Methodist lay preachers, and therefore fluent and confident.

The Tolpuddle Martyrs were immediately dispatched to Australia, and just as quickly opposition to their transportation began. 30,000 demonstrators marched with a petition to the Home Secretary, and other petitions and protests followed. Protest was largely in London and the North, with little from Dorset.

James Frampton, the magistrate who had prosecuted the Tolpuddle men, now refused to grant any parish money to the families left behind, telling them that the Union Club must support them. This refusal was illegal. A fund was raised from northern unions to support the families, and relief arrived quickly and the wives were able to help others in Tolpuddle. One of the labourers who earnt only 10s a week with his two sons had been receiving 3s 6d from the parish to support his five other children, 'but now the 3s 6d is taken from them, because he was in the Union, and for a week past they had had but only one meal a day, and now this day he is obliged to give up work, being so weak and bad for want of food, but we have relieved them a little' (letter written by the wives, April 1834, Dorset County Library).

In 1836 the men were pardoned, but they did not get back to England until 1838. George Loveless immediately produced a pamphlet about the trial (and the horrors of transportation) which sold more than 12,000 copies in a few months.

Even though the Tolpuddle Martyrs were pardoned, their trial and transportation had had the effect the Government wanted: trade

A contemporary drawing of some of the Tolpuddle Martyrs after they had been brought back from Australia in 1838.

unionism amongst the agricultural labourers virtually ceased to exist. Wages were as low as ever, and the many Friendly Societies which were continuing to flourish and expand were limited to being mutual insurance societies against illness, rather than proper Unions.

Two of the Tolpuddle Martyrs took part in what turned out to be the last attempt at Agricultural Trades Unions in Dorset for a generation. In 1838 the newly formed Chartists were holding meetings all over the country to gather support. They were successful in the north. In November 1838 a meeting was organised at Charlton Down, near Blandford. Placards were displayed all over the county, many of them advertising George Loveless's support for the meeting, and another of the Tolpuddle men, John Standfield, was present at the meeting.

Probably as many as 1,500 people attended the meeting, to hear several Chartist speakers enumerating their six points: universal male suffrage; payment for MPs; equal electoral districts; annual parliaments; no property qualifications for MPs and the secret ballot. Joining a Union was also part of the message, and many Dorset labourers did become members.

Those who joined the Union paid for it. A correspondence in the *Chronicle* includes accusations from one of the Chartist organisers that labourers had been sacked for joining the Union, naming the farmers involved. One replied, and he had indeed sacked eight men for joining the Union, but they had come to their senses, left the Union and been re-employed 'with the exception of one young man, who being impertinent, I told him to go about his business'. In Blandford the Poor Law Guardians were refusing to help those who had been sacked because they joined the Union, and so the men gave in.

The *Chronicle*'s editorial for 17th January 1839 concedes that some labourers in Dorset were not receiving enough money and 'the labourers of Dorsetshire, having nobly withstood the dangerous seductions exercised by the agitators who recently came amongst them, and proved that they well know that their best interest lies in maintaining a good feeling between themselves and their employers, thus deserve that investigation into their condition which will serve to ascertain whether in all parts they do receive that amount of wages to which they may be considered as fairly entitled'.

No such investigation took place, the Union failed, and things only got worse for the labourers in the 1840s. In 1844 a Government report stated that in Dorset 'wages are so low, that they cannot fall [and the labourers] normal state is one of the deepest privation, to lower which would depopulate the land'.

The trial and subsequent pardon of the Tolpuddle Martyrs put Dorset at the centre of national attention. Conflict between the rapidly growing Trades Union movement and government was inevitable but it happened in Dorset because of two men. James Frampton JP thought that Unions were wicked and would lead to revolution: George Loveless, an articulate labourer, thought Unions were the only hope for the workers to earn a living wage. One was opposing riots, the other pushing for reform. In effect, both men won. Frampton frightened the labourers of Dorset, and no Union was established for labourers in the county. Nationally Trades Unions managed to get the Martyrs' conviction overturned by orchestrating huge protests. If they had not succeeded all Unions could have been considered illegal.

# THE REGENCY LEGACY

Physically there are many legacies within Dorset from the earlier nineteenth century. From the refined terraces of Weymouth, through many coaching inns to the many farms and mills rebuilt at the time, it is hard to travel far in the county without seeing buildings of the period. Less obviously, much of the landscape was altered – some by enclosure, and some by tree-planting or draining.

The period 1800-1838 sees the start of much of modern world, with the principal of electing official bodies like Parliament or councils; the start of universal education; reform of the penal system; the emergence of the middle class; and the removal of official religious restrictions.

Ironically the most famous event of the period – the trial and subsequent pardon of the Tolpuddle Martyrs – saw the defeat of those who were hoping for reform. Although the Martyrs were pardoned and returned from transportation, they did not succeed in improving pay or the conditions of agricultural labourers in the county, nor did they succeed in setting up an agricultural Trades Union.

The upper classes of Dorset were probably happy simply to have survived without a revolution in England. Many of them had feared that the country would revolt in the 1820s or 30s, a time when many European countries suffered revolution. The reforms of the period, helped by the stability produced amongst the labourers by non-conformist sects like Methodism, defused the situation. The song sung at the 1831 election in Blandford was right:

> *And if we do not have Reform*
> *We'll have a Revolution*

England had reform, not revolution, but there had been riots along the way in Dorset.

# FURTHER READING

From 1800 there was a huge increase in printing, so there are many more pamphlets and books, and larger local newspapers. The printed sources for the period are thus very rich. All un-referenced quotations are from *The Dorset County Chronicle* which was founded in Dorchester in 1823. Many travel books and government reports describe the county.

William Barnes poems about the labourers are to be found in *Poems of Rural Life in the Dorset Dialect* (1844), and the story about milking time and music in Barbara Kerr's *Bound to the Soil* (1968, p.17). Sir Frederick Morton Eden's accounts of the labourers is from *The State of the Poor: A History of the Labouring Classes in England* (ed. A.G. L. Roberts, 1928).

William Stevenson's *General View of the Agriculture of the County of Dorset* (1815) and the four volumes of the Second Edition of Hutchins' *History and Antiquities of the County of Dorset* (1796-1815) have been used extensively.

The best account of the Tolpuddle Martyrs is George Loveless' *The Victims of Whiggery* (1837 or 8), but *The Dorchester Labourers* (as the Tolpuddle Martyrs were known at the time) by J.A. Roebuck (c. 1835) adds detail.

*The Journals of Mary Frampton* (1885); *Memoires and Traditions* by Lucia Boswell Stone (1895); Robert Southey (published as by Don Manuel Espriella) *Letters from England* (1808); *A Walk on the Coast of Dorsetshire from Lyme to Lulworth* (1828) by T. H. Williams; *The Personal Notebooks of Thomas Hardy* (ed. Richard H. Taylor, 1978), and John Pennie *The Tale of a Modern Genius* (1827) give many contemporary details as does *Methodism in Dorset* (1870) by John S. Simon.

Pamphlets used include the Annual Reports of the National Society (Schools) for the early 19th century (DCL); *Minutes of Evidence before a select Committee of the House of Lords . . .* (1835) and *A Letter to D.O.P. Okeden* together with an inquiry into the merits of his Poor Law Report (1839) both by H.F. Yeatman; *A Letter to the Members of Parliament for Dorsetshire on the subject of poor Relief and Labourers' Wages* by D.O.P. Okeden (1830); *Practical Retrenchment the Legitimate Object of Reform* (c.1833) by John Penny. Coaches are taken from *Dorchester and its Environs* (1832) by James Savage.

'The Dorset by-election of 1831' by Richard Morris *Proceedings of the Dorset Natural History and Archaelogical Society* 109 (1987) 5-16; 'The

Agricultural Riots in Dorset in 1830' by W.H. Parry Okeden, same journal
vol. 51 (1930) 75-95; 'Some German Reflections on Dorset' by G. Lanning
*Somerset and Dorset Notes and Queries* vol. 33, 273-5 and *The Island and
Royal Manor of Portland* by J.H. Bettey (1970).

All the following are in the Dorset County Museum: the Symondsbury
Friendly Society Rules; the Holy Trinity, Dorchester, church poster (Dorset
Album); the Reform poems (Ship Album vol. 1); and the copy of *Chronicles
of Cranborne Chase* with manuscript additions.

# ACKNOWLEDGEMENTS

---

I am grateful to Christopher Chaplin for his encouragement while writing
this; to Sheena Pearce for her typing of it; to Dr Joe Bettey for reading it;
and to the Dorset County Museum and the Dorset County Library for all the
material in their care.

I would like to thank the following for allowing the inclusion of illustra-
tions in their possession or for which they hold the copyright. Cecil N.
Cullingford: page 17; Dorset Natural History and Achaeological Society:
pages 12, 13, 19 (top), 28 (right), 51 (both), 55; Eric Garrett: page 43;
National Portrait Gallery: page 45; Jonathan North: pages 11, 23, 53; Royal
Commission Historical Monuments (England), © Crown Copyright: fron-
tispiece, pages 14 (top), 18, 20, 26, 29, 36, 37, 40, 41, 44, 59, 63, 66 (top), 66
(bottom).

*The*

# DISCOVER DORSET

*Series of Books*

A series of paperback books providing informative illustrated
introductions to Dorset's history, culture and way of life.
The following titles have so far been published.

BRIDGES *David McFetrich and Jo Parsons*

CASTLES AND FORTS *Colin Pomeroy*

CRANBORNE CHASE *Desmond Hawkins*

FARMING *J.H.Bettey*

FOLLIES *Jonathan Holt*

FOSSILS *Richard Edmonds*

GEOLOGY *Paul Ensom*

THE GEORGIANS *Jo Draper*

THE INDUSTRIAL PAST *Peter Stanier*

ISLE OF PURBECK *Paul Hyland*

LEGENDS *Jeremy Harte*

MILLS *Peter Stanier*

PORTLAND *Stuart Morris*

POTTERY *Penny Copland-Griffiths*

THE PREHISTORIC AGE *Bill Putnam*

REGENCY, RIOT AND REFORM *Jo Draper*

THE ROMANS *Bill Putnam*

SAXONS AND VIKINGS *David Hinton*

SHIPWRECKS *Maureen Attwooll*

STONE QUARRYING *Jo Thomas*

THE VICTORIANS *Jude James*

All the books about Dorset published by The Dovecote Press
are available in bookshops throughout the county,
or in case of difficulty direct from the publishers.
The Dovecote Press Ltd, Stanbridge,
Wimborne, Dorset BH21 4JD
Tel: 01258 840549  www.dovecotepress.com